A Thousand Sentences

Caleb Gattegno

Educational Solutions Worldwide Inc.

First published in the United States of America in 1974. Reprinted in 1981. Reprinted in 1993. Reprinted in 2010.

Educational Solutions Worldwide Inc.
2nd Floor 99 University Place, New York, N.Y. 10003-4555
www.EducationalSolutions.com

Table of Contents

Preface 1

My House 3

Eating 4

On Bedrooms 7

The Living Room 10

In the Kitchen 11

In and Around the House 14

Outside the House 17

Jobs and Professions 23

Education 27

Family Relationships 28

Holidays and Anniversaries 32

Driving and Transportation 35

On Taxis 39

Theater and Entertainment 41

Music and Concerts 44

Writing and Painting 48

Toiletry and Beauty Care 50

Clothing 53

The Armed Forces 56

Navigation 58

Traveling 60

Standard of Living 61

The State 63

Agriculture 66

Sports 69

Immigration 73

Working at Night 74

Seas and Rivers 76

Cleaning and Laundry 78

Relaxation 79

Feelings 82

Accidents and Wounds 83

On Bees and Wax 85

Smoking 86

Drinking 88

Trains and Stations 90

Shopping 93

Post Offices and Mail 95

Telephone 98

Correspondence 100

News and the Press 102

On Laughter 103

Money 105

Animals and Pets 108

The Future 110

Preface

The sentences in this book are generally short in length and direct in expression. They aim to provide a first exercise for students who are not ready to read a whole book in the English language. At the same time the sentences are designed to convey a picture of some aspects of social and cultural life in the United States.

Although the sentences have been constructed in such a way that the meanings of some words can be inferred from the context, a printed text cannot by itself guarantee that it will be understood by all readers. Teachers who use this book will find that it is most effective when used in conjunction with visual materials - for example, The Silent Way wall pictures, newspapers and magazines. The organization of the subject matter covered by the sentences, fanning out from the home to the larger technological society, facilitates the selection of suitable materials.

It is not imperative to follow the sequence of the book. Students can be invited to begin with those sections that are most accessible to them, or that are of topical or personal interest for them, and compile their own associated materials so that they gather the vocabulary that relates to this area of experience. With such a flexible approach the use of a dictionary will fall into place, as an additional but not primary means of coming to terms with the English language.

My House

1   I live in a house.

2   There are six rooms in my house.

3   The dining room is one of them.

4   Three of the others are bedrooms.

5   There is a living room and a kitchen.

6   There is also a bathroom.

7   We have most of our meals in the dining room.

8   In the morning we have breakfast in the kitchen.

9   We sleep in the bedrooms.

10   In the living room we talk together, listen to music, read or watch television.

11   We also entertain our guests there.

12   In the bathroom there is a bathtub, a shower, a sink, and a toilet.

13   In the dining room there are a table and six chairs and a buffet along the wall.

14   On the buffet there is a clock and sometimes a vase of flowers.

15   In the buffet we keep the plates, glasses, knives, and forks.

16   The plates are made of china.

17   The dinner plates are big and round; the bread and butter plates are round too, but smaller; there are bowls for soup, and cups and saucers for tea and coffee. All together these plates are called a dinner service.

18   The glasses are of different shapes and sizes for different drinks.

Eating

19   Some people like to have a light breakfast, but others, especially those who do physical work, eat a good meal in the morning.

20   Breakfast often begins with a glass of fruit juice.

21 This may be followed by cereal with milk and sugar.

22 In winter people often eat hot cereal.

23 The United States produces many cereals: wheat, corn, oats, barley, bran, etc.

24 Many people eat eggs for breakfast.

25 They are cooked in various ways and are often served with bacon or sausages.

26 Those who have a light breakfast may have only coffee and toast or a roll or a pastry.

27 The toast is served hot with butter and usually with jam as well.

28 Most Americans drink coffee with their breakfast, but some prefer tea or milk.

29 The two main meals of the day are lunch and dinner.

30 Eating customs vary throughout the United States.

31 This is partly because of climate and partly because different parts of the country have been influenced by the customs that foreigners have brought with them.

32   Italian, French, Jewish, Chinese, and Greek cultures are among those which have greatly influenced American eating habits.

33   In general, Americans are meat eaters.

34   The U.S. produces excellent beef, lamb, and pork.

35   Poultry, especially turkey, is also eaten on such holidays as Thanksgiving and Christmas.

36   Fried chicken is an everyday dish, particularly in the South.

37   Fish, and especially shellfish, are also very popular.

38   Two American dishes that have become famous are the hamburger and the hot dog.

39   These days most foods can be bought frozen.

40   Dinner is in the evening and is usually the meal that the whole family eats together.

41   Sometimes dinner begins with a salad or, in winter, with soup.

42   Then comes the main dish, meat or fish with vegetables.

43   The third course is dessert, which may be hot or cold.

44   Ice cream, cheesecake or apple pie are popular desserts.

45   Ice cream is an American specialty, and one can find many different flavors.

46   Some Americans drink wine with dinner; there is usually ice water and some other beverage served with meals, especially in restaurants.

47   Children drink milk, juice, or water with their meals.

On Bedrooms

48   There are double beds for two people, single beds for one person, and cribs for babies.

49   People in bed lie on the mattress.

50   The mattress rests on a spring base.

51   Some modern mattresses have springs inside them, and others are made of foam.

52   The bedding consists of two sheets, one or more blankets, and one or two pillows in pillow cases.

53   When it is very cold, a quilt is sometimes added.

54   A bedspread is sometimes put over the bed (during the day).

55   Beside the bed there may be a night table.

56   On this night table there is usually a reading lamp and perhaps an alarm clock and something to read.

57   Against the walls are a dressing table and a chest of drawers.

58   Clothes are hung in the closets.

59   Closets are wardrobes built into the walls.

60   Underwear, handkerchiefs, stockings, socks, gloves, etc., are kept in drawers.

61   At the bottom of the closet one puts shoes, boots, sandals, sneakers, and slippers.

62   At the top of a closet there is often a shelf for hats.

63   On the dressing table are toiletries: hairbrushes, combs, perfumes, powders, etc.

64   Usually there is a mirror attached either to the dressing table or to the back of a closet door.

65   In front of the dressing table there is a chair or stool.

66   On the floor there may be a rug or carpet.

67   In addition to the reading lamp on the night table, there may be a ceiling light or other lamps in the bedroom.

68   The light switch for one of these is usually on the wall near the door.

69   There may be another near the bed or on the wall behind the bed.

70   At night we sleep.

71   We wake up in the morning.

72   Sometimes we need the alarm clock to wake us.

73   After getting up we use the bathroom to wash or shave.

74   Then we have breakfast.

75   After breakfast those who must go to work or school leave.

The Living Room

76   After returning from work we have dinner, and then we go into the living room.

77   In the living room there is a radio or a sound system and a television set.

78   There are also armchairs and a couch.

79   Armchairs are more comfortable than straight-backed chairs.

80   They are softer and more inviting.

81   A couch has some features of an armchair and some of a bed.

82   A couch is like two or three armchairs joined together, with arms only at the ends, or like a bed with a back.

83   When we have visitors we take them into the living room.

84   If there is a piano in the house, it will also be in the living room.

85   There may be a coffee table in the living room and other small tables, called end tables, for serving coffee or

drinks. There may be ashtrays on them for people who smoke.

86   Sometimes we dance there.

87   Sometimes we play cards there as well.

88   We listen to music on the radio or on a sound system.

89   The living room and the dining room are used by the whole family.

In the Kitchen

90   The kitchen is an indispensable room; meals are prepared in the kitchen and food is kept there.

91   The stove on which one cooks may be fueled by gas or electricity.

92   Pots and pans are put on the burners.

93   Cooking utensils are often made of wood, aluminum, or plastic.

94   Pot holders and oven mitts prevent one from getting burned while preparing meals.

95 Different kinds of dishes are used in the oven than on the burners.

96 The sink, with hot and cold water faucets, is usually built into one of the counters.

97 After being washed, the dishes are left on the counter to drain.

98 There are cabinets and shelves in the kitchen.

99 Things that are used often must be easily accessible.

100 A number of utensils are kept in the kitchen drawers. They are used for cutting meat or vegetables, for peeling or grating fruit or vegetables, for beating eggs and cream, for squeezing lemons and oranges, for opening cans, and for serving different dishes.

101 These days there are also a number of modern electrical appliances for the kitchen.

102 The mixer is one of these appliances and it has many uses.

103 Preparing soups and making cakes and other desserts is much easier since the invention of the mixer.

104 Many modern kitchens have electric dishwashers.

105   On the counters we prepare the food for cooking, and meals are often served there.

106   Somewhere in the kitchen there is a garbage pail, a recycling bin, and sometimes a compost bucket.

107   The compost bucket is for the parts of the food that we do not eat, such as vegetable peelings, fruit pits, etc.

108   The garbage pail is emptied into the big trash can outside.

109   The trash can is emptied by the garbage trucks driven by municipal workers.

110   This way the garbage is destroyed and the houses are kept clean and pleasant to live in.

111   In buildings where many people live there may be a garbage chute for disposing of trash.

112   Every kitchen has a refrigerator to keep food fresh.

113   In the refrigerator we keep vegetables, meat, butter, milk, cream, eggs, cheese, and drinks which need to be served cold.

114   In the top part of the refrigerator there is often a freezer compartment, which is very cold.

115   In the freezer we make ice, and we also keep frozen foods and ice cream.

116   Although one cooks standing up, there is often a table in the kitchen, and chairs or stools at one of the counters.

In and Around the House

117   In a house where several people live, one finds many objects of different sizes which are used for different things

118   Rugs, carpets, linoleum, rubber, or wooden boards cover the floors of the rooms.

119   Pictures, engravings, photographs, or tapestries are hung on the walls.

120   Mirrors are sometimes hung on the walls too, sometimes for use and sometimes just for decoration or to reflect light.

121   Drapes and curtains are hung in front of the windows.

122   Slipcovers are sometimes put on armchairs and couches.

123   Hat racks and coat stands are placed near the front door, though these have more commonly been replaced by a coat closet.

124   Lights are attached to ceilings or walls, and lamps are placed on tables or on the floor.

125   Bath towels and hand towels are found in the bathroom.

126   Outside the front door a mat is placed so that people can wipe their shoes before entering a house.

127   A dwelling is a place where one lives.

128   It is usually called one's home.

129   In cities, most people live in apartments.

130   In the country or the suburbs homes are much larger, and may be houses of more than one story.

131   In this case a house might have a basement below ground level and an attic under the roof. There are stairs for going from one story to another.

132   Apartment buildings have elevators and stairs.

133   There is often a garden around the house.

134   Flowers, trees, and shrubs are usually in front of the house.

135   There is often a backyard behind the house.

136   Some people plant a vegetable garden in their backyard.

137   Sometimes there are plants climbing on the fences or on part of the house; they are called vines.

138   The lawn is the part of the yard planted with grass, which is cut regularly.

139   Lawns and gardens demand a great deal of care.

140   Looking after a garden requires a lot of time and patience.

141   Not everyone makes a good gardener.

142   Successful gardeners are said to have a "green thumb."

143   In the country, one property may be separated from another by a fence or hedge.

144   A property may have a gate which opens onto the street; sometimes there is no fence in front of the house and the garden ends at the sidewalk.

Outside the House

145   Houses are connected by streets and together form a town or a city.

146   Streets are maintained by municipal governments.

147   Roads form a network connecting the different places in a country; they are maintained by the state or the nation.

148   These days automobiles make many places more accessible than they were in former times.

149   Automobiles require good roads.

150   In the U.S., well constructed roads, often called thruways, link most of the major cities around the country.

151   Thanks to this modern system of highways, surface transportation from one part of the country to another has become very easy and popular.

152   Almost every family living in the suburbs owns at least one car.

153   Most suburban houses have a garage or a carport.

154   In the cities it is difficult to keep a car because of the problem of parking and garaging it.

155   Garages in the cities are often underground.

156   In some places cars may be left in the street overnight but usually must be removed early in the morning.

157   Some people, especially those living in the cities, use only public transportation.

158   A group of houses in the country is called a town.

159   In the United States one can find very small towns and enormous cities.

160   In the city of New York there are more than eight million people.

161   Sometimes a city has a natural boundary, for example, if it is on an island or beside a river.

162   In Manhattan these natural boundaries have forced the city to grow upwards.

163   Very tall buildings are called skyscrapers.

164   Small country towns have only one main street, often called Main Street, but in cities there are many streets connecting the various sections.

165   The sections of a city where people live are called residential areas.

166   Even in these areas one can find big department stores.

167   The department stores sell almost anything one can think of.

168   Apart from the department stores there are also big shops which specialize in certain goods:

169   For example, clothing stores and tailors where one can buy clothes made to measure;

170   Jewelers, where one finds jewelry: ornaments made of gold or silver, usually decorated with precious stones;

171   Milliners, where only hats are made and sold (there are few of these nowadays);

172   Art galleries, where there are exhibitions of paintings, sculpture, pottery, ceramics or other works of art for sale;

173   Antique shops and furniture stores, where one can buy old or new things to furnish one's house;

174   Travel agencies, banks and insurance offices;

175   Car sales rooms and auto rental agencies;

176   Hardware stores where one can find paint, tools, utensils, etc.

177   Apart from business concerns, there are also various museums;

178   Theaters where one can see modern or classical plays;

179   Movie theaters, where they show both foreign and American films;

180   One or several zoos, where animals from many countries are kept;

181   One or more botanical gardens, where there are many species of plants, local and foreign, sometimes even very rare specimens.

182   There are also various academic establishments: universities, schools and colleges;

183   Public and municipal buildings, such as libraries and the city hall.

184   There are parks and public gardens where one can walk or sit or play.

185   In each state in the United States there is a capital city.

186   In the capital cities there is a capitol building, which houses the government offices and the legislative houses.

187   There are also military installations, police stations, and fire stations.

188   In almost every city one can see monuments commemorating famous people or historical events.

189   In the cities public transportation is provided by buses and trains: trains which run underground are called subways.

190   In some cities one can travel by helicopter, especially to and from the airports.

191   Airports are often constructed near cities, but some are quite a distance away.

192   In most cities there are one or more railroad stations.

193   There may be special stations for long distance trains and others for local, suburban or interstate travel.

194   A suburb is a residential area close to a city, which may have its own local government.

195   The inhabitants of the cities form the urban population.

196   People who live in the country and on farms form the rural populations.

197   City life is very different from country life.

198   Most city inhabitants live in apartments in large buildings, some of which are so big that hundreds of families live there.

199   Living this way, one rarely gets to meet one's neighbors.

200   In the country, however, neighbors know each other well and have common interests.

201   In order to get fresh air and exercise, the inhabitants of the cities go for walks in the parks or leave the city on weekends.

202   On the other hand, they can find anything they want in the stores and do not have to produce it.

203   Most industry in the United States is on the outskirts of the cities.

204   This has caused many problems because of pollution of the air, the rivers and the sea.

Jobs and Professions

205   The people in cities who work in offices are called white-collar workers.

206   People who work in factories or who do physical labor are called blue-collar workers.

207   Anyone who works for someone else is called an employee.

208   People who work for the government are called civil servants.

209   Some civil servants are police officers, customs officers, immigration officers, etc.

210   Fire fighters are people who fight fires and other natural disasters.

211   A person who owns their own business or who controls a business is commonly known as the boss.

212　In a business there are directors, assistant directors and executives who direct the affairs of the various departments.

213　Those who are concerned with accounts, taxes, and the financial side of a business are called accountants.

214　In factories the person in charge of a section is called a foreman.

215　The technical director in a factory is an engineer.

216　The title "head" or "chief" is given to various people in charge of different sections of a business or factory. There are heads of divisions, chief engineers, chiefs of staff, and so on.

217　The word "manager" is used for a person who is in charge of a business which he or she does not own.

218　Corporations are managed by a Board of Directors. Their leader, the Chairman of the Board, presides at meetings.

219　Those who sell their products directly to the public are called merchants.

220　There are special names for different merchants.

221　Flower merchants are called florists.

222   Fruit and vegetable merchants do not sell their own produce; they buy from the farmers at wholesale markets.

223   The person who sells meat is the butcher.

224   He also buys his meat at a market. These markets are open very early in the morning.

225   A grocer sells foods in packages, cans, jars, and bottles, as well as fresh fruit and vegetables.

226   These foods may be domestic or imported. In some groceries one can still buy things loose, which means they have not been pre-packaged.

227   Bakeries sell bread, rolls, and sometimes cakes and pastries as well.

228   Candy, chocolates, and other sweet things are sold at the candy store.

229   There are also delicatessens which sell hot and cold meats, milk, butter, cheese, sausages and often foods cooked and ready to eat.

230   There are liquor stores, which sell wines and spirits.

231   Today many small food stores are disappearing and are being replaced by chains of supermarkets, which sell all kinds of food.

232   There is a supermarket in almost every shopping center.

233   Large department stores and discount stores are replacing small specialty shops.

234   The old trades are giving way to mass production.

235   There are very few milliners left who make and sell their own hats;

236   Or corset-makers who make corsets;

237   Or launderers who wash clothes.

238   These days many people either own their own automatic washing machines or use public machines in places called laundromats.

239   Most winter clothing cannot be hand-washed and is usually sent to the dry-cleaners.

240   There are still men and women who have a trade, but they rarely work alone or have their own businesses.

241   Dentists, attorneys, accountants, and architects are perhaps the last examples, and their jobs are not called trades, but professions.

242   Doctors are also professional people. The family doctor still exists, but modern hospitals and clinics have made the job more general. Many doctors nowadays work together in a medical center, rather than having their own practice.

243   The progress of modern technology has influenced all human activity and is changing the face of the world.

Education

244   Elementary schools may include a kindergarten class and sometimes even a pre-kindergarten for children of four years or younger.

245   Elementary schools in the United States generally end at the sixth grade, but in some states they go up to the eighth grade, while in others the fifth grade is the last grade.

246   In some of those states there are junior high schools for grades 6-8 and then high schools for grades 9-12

247   Secondary schools follow elementary schools. Those which prepare one for a trade are called vocational schools.

248   Everyone who attends school is called a student.

249   Universities generally select their students from among the high school graduates.

250   Every state maintains a public university as well as public high schools and elementary schools.

251   In addition to these there are also private schools for all age groups, including private universities and colleges.

Family Relationships

252   The members of a family living at one time may belong to three and sometimes even four generations.

253   The youngest member of a family may be a baby.

254   "Child" and "baby" are words which apply to both sexes; that is, a child or a baby can be either a boy or a girl.

255   At about twelve or thirteen, the time of puberty, a child becomes an adolescent.

256   A male is called a boy until about seventeen, and then he is called a young man.

257   A female is called a girl till she is thirteen or fourteen, and then, a young woman.

258   In the United States, many young people refer to themselves and are referred to as "kids."

259   This last word is slang, that is, language which is popular among a group.

260   The group may include a whole nation, as is the case with the word "kid."

261   A child has a father and a mother who are his parents.

262   Parents may have several children. Parents and children make up a family in the strict sense of the word.

263   The boys in the family are the sons of their parents and the brothers of the other children in the family. The girls are the daughters of their parents and the sisters of the other children.

264   All the people who have an ancestor in common are called relatives. They belong to one family in the broad sense.

265   The father and mother of your father are your paternal grandparents, and the father and mother of your mother are your maternal grandparents. They make up the third generation counting back.

266   When I address my grandmother, I say "Grandma," and when I address my grandfather, I say "Grandpa."

267   They call me by my first name.

268   Many children have pet names for their grandparents.

269   To my mother I say "Mom" or "Mommy," and to my father I say "Dad" or "Daddy."

270   My grandparents' parents are my great-grandparents. They make the fourth generation counting back from me. I am their great-grandchild.

271   My mother's and father's brothers and sisters are my uncles and aunts. I call their wives and husbands "aunt" and "uncle" too.

272   I am their nephew. If I were a girl, I would be their niece.

273   The brothers of my grandparents are my great-uncles, and my grandparents' sisters are my great-aunts.

274   I am their great-nephew. If I were a girl, I would be their great-niece.

275   My uncles' and aunts' children are my first cousins.

276   In general, all more distant relatives are called cousins also.

277   A man and a woman who are united in legal matrimony are married.

278   Thus, they are a married couple or partners in marriage.

279   He refers to her as his wife, and she calls him her husband.

280   In legal terminology they are each other's spouse.

281   The parents of one partner are the in-laws of the other partner, the father-in-law and the mother-in-law.

282   The husband is the son-in-law of his wife's parents, and she is the daughter-in-law of his parents.

283   The brothers and sisters of one partner are the brothers-in-law and sisters-in-law of the other partner.

284 The parents of one's husband or wife may be called by their first names, or Mother and Father, or even Mom and Dad or Mr. and Mrs. ....

285 Family links are more important in some parts of the United States than in others. After a person is grown-up or married, he or she usually does not live with his or her parents.

Holidays and Anniversaries

286 The whole family celebrates the days which mark each year the anniversaries of the births of its members. These are birthdays.

287 Other events in life are also celebrated.

288 Wedding anniversaries are honored each year, but particularly after twenty-five years of marriage, which is the silver anniversary; after fifty years, the golden anniversary; and after sixty years, the diamond anniversary.

289 Families in the United States also celebrate Mother's Day in May and Father's Day in June.

290 Apart from family celebrations there are national holidays, and religious holidays which are observed by the whole country.

291 On July 4, Americans celebrate the anniversary of their national independence.

292 Veterans' Day and Memorial Day honor those who fought and died for their country.

293 The birthdays of Abraham Lincoln, sixteenth president of the United States, and George Washington, first president of the United States, are celebrated in February, and that of Martin Luther King, in January.

294 Labor Day in the United States is on the first Monday in September.

295 October 12 is Columbus Day, which honors Christopher Columbus' arrival in America in 1492.

296 Thanksgiving is an important national holiday. It falls on the fourth Thursday in November and commemorates the feast shared by the Pilgrims, the first settlers in New England, and the Indians, the original inhabitants.

297 Thanksgiving is a family holiday and people often travel long distances to be together with their parents and brothers and sisters at this time.

298   Christmas, which falls on December 25, is also a time for family reunions.

299   New Year's Day is the first day of January; it is also a public holiday.

300   Easter is a moveable feast; Good Friday, Easter Day and Easter Monday are public holidays in some countries.

301   On the eve of All Saints' Day, that is, on October 31, Halloween is celebrated, especially by children, who dress up as ghosts, witches, skeletons, etc.

302   There are also local religious and historical holidays in different regions of the country.

303   Annual vacations for working people vary according to the state, the unions, the particular job, and the length of time they have worked at the same job.

304   On vacation many people like to visit their families, especially if they live in a different part of the country.

305   Long distances can be covered quite quickly, thanks to the Interstate Highway system.

306   En route people may stay in motels, which are located all along these roads.

307 Either a motel has its own restaurant, or there is one nearby.

308 Some motels have swimming pools for their guests' use.

309 Each room has a bed, a desk, a dressing table, a telephone, and a television set; usually there is a private bathroom.

310 For a vacation one might go to the beach or to the mountains; nowadays more and more people are going abroad during their vacation.

311 Students and teachers get the longest summer vacation: two or three months, from June until September.

312 They also have time off at Christmas and in the spring.

Driving and Transportation

313 The roads in America today are very crowded with cars, trucks, and buses.

314 There are also a variety of bicycles, some with motors and some without.

315   There are interstate highways going from one state to another.

316   Highways are wide roads, often divided in the middle by trees or a low fence, with two or more lanes going in each direction.

317   In the United States one drives on the right.

318   In the cities red and green traffic lights regulate the traffic; there may also be an amber light which cautions the driver that the lights are about to change.

319   The United States produces a lot of cars, but one can also see many foreign cars on the roads.

320   Before being allowed to drive a car, a person must obtain a license.

321   Driving regulations vary somewhat from state to state; in most states one may obtain a license at sixteen.

322   Driving schools can prepare one for the test. One may also have to attend a lecture on road regulations, and receive instruction for night driving, highway driving and driving in wet or snowy conditions.

323   The test includes an examination on the highway code and road signs and a practical examination in driving a

car. For the practical examination one must be able to drive forwards and backwards, turn, pass another car, change gear, brake, and park as instructed.

324 Nowadays most cars have an automatic transmission, and there is no need to change gear, except when reversing and parking.

325 Traffic police and highway patrollers are authorized to give tickets to drivers who break the speed limit or any other traffic regulation.

326 Tickets can be given for parking or traffic violations.

327 A ticket is a fine which may be appealed in court.

328 There are speed limits on the highways as well as in the cities.

329 Highways are also called turnpikes, freeways, thruways, and parkways, depending on how they were planned and funded.

330 Many highways in the United States are toll roads, which means one must pay a sum after traveling certain distances. This money is used for the maintenance of the road.

331 Some highways have gas stations on "islands" in the middle of the road or on one side so that one can get gas without leaving the highway.

332 Interstate highways are limited access roads; this means one can only enter or leave the highway via ramps along the road.

333 One can fly or take a bus to most towns in the United States; in some parts of the country one can also take a train.

334 For this one must buy a ticket. By taking a train one also avoids worrying about traffic, weather conditions, tolls and gas.

335 One buys a token instead of a ticket for subway trains.

336 These are put in a slot which allows one to pass through a turnstile onto the platform.

337 One can buy several tokens at a time and therefore not have to wait in line each time and perhaps miss a train.

338 In most cities one pays the same price for a token no matter how far one is going on the subway.

339 In some places a subway token may be used on a city bus.

On Taxis

340   Taxis are public vehicles for one person or for groups of up to four people.

341   Taxis are also called cabs, a name coming from the original horse-drawn carriages for hire.

342   In the city, taxis have a meter to indicate the amount to be paid for each ride.

343   For trips outside the city the rate is fixed before setting out.

344   The driver usually expects a tip; it is a percentage of the amount shown on the meter.

345   This percentage varies with the generosity of the passenger. In general, it is about 15%.

346   Some taxi companies have a central office which maintains constant radio contact with their drivers.

347   This makes service easy and quick and enables one to telephone for a taxi.

348   Other taxi companies have drivers who cruise around the streets waiting to be hailed.

349 At rush hours, or when it is raining, it can be very difficult to find a taxi.

350 To hail a taxi in the street one often has to shout loudly or wave or whistle.

351 When traffic is heavy, it often happens that an inexperienced driver causes a traffic jam.

352 In many of the large cities most streets are one-way only.

353 In major cities there are many intersections and squares where several streets converge.

354 Rotaries, also called traffic circles, slow up the traffic but make driving less dangerous; they make it possible for cars from several converging roads to cross without trouble.

355 Usually there are no police officers at rotaries, and the drivers organize themselves according to the rules of the road.

356 Courtesy is also needed on these occasions.

Theater and Entertainment

357　A theater is a large hall where the public, after buying a ticket, is admitted to watch a play.

358　Most tickets are good for a single performance only.

359　The cheapest seats are those farthest from the stage.

360　Orchestra seats, boxes, and lower balconies cost more, but the seats are more comfortable and afford a better view.

361　One is given a program, which contains information about the play, the order of the acts, the author and the actors.

362　There are sometimes photos of the principal actors or scenes in the program.

363　There are always advertisements in these programs.

364　Plays can be comedies, dramas or tragedies.

365　Comedies are usually gay and amusing.

366　In a tragedy the hero is a victim of his destiny.

367 In tragedies the heroes struggle against forces stronger than themselves and, invariably, lose.

368 A drama is a portrayal of human conflict.

369 Actors perform on a stage.

370 Backstage there is a prompter, who comes to the aid of actors who forget their lines.

371 The curtain rises at the beginning of a play and comes down at the end of each act.

372 Footlights and spotlights are used to light the stage according to the director's instructions.

373 In classical theater or in plays where the action takes place in the past, actors dress in the style of the period.

374 Actors wear heavy make-up on stage.

375 The author and the director determine how a play will be staged.

376 New York City is the theatrical center of the United States. The theater district is called Broadway.

377 Musical comedies are a very popular form of Broadway theater; they are often very lavish productions.

378   Repertory theaters are common in smaller communities, especially near college campuses.

379   One can also go to the opera or the ballet if one likes singing or dancing.

380   These take place in large rooms, usually with the audience facing a stage.

381   In movie theaters the stage is taken up by a screen.

382   Modern screens are huge and rectangular or even parabolic in shape.

383   Movies are motion pictures shown in theaters.

384   The original movies were called "Silents" because they had no sound track; they didn't have dialogue, music, or even color.

385   There are adventure movies, documentaries, dramas, detective movies, historical and biblical movies, love stories, etc.

386   It is polite to turn off your cell phone before you enter any theater.

387   Before the movie begins, short scenes from upcoming films, called previews or trailers, are shown.

388 In the cities one can sometimes see two full-length movies, called a double feature, at the same show. These are often old movies which are still popular.

389 The invention of television has brought the movies into every home.

390 A television set has a fluorescent screen on which the picture is formed.

391 Now that the internet has appeared, the availability of TV programs is even wider.

392 Whether attending a performance in a theater or watching television at home, one is involved in the unfolding of a plot.

Music and Concerts

393 At a symphony concert the musicians play their instruments under the direction of a conductor.

394 The string instruments in the orchestra are the violin, the viola, the cello, and the bass.

395 Usually the pianist plays a grand piano at a concert.

396 The wind instruments are of two kinds: the woodwinds, for example, the flute, the oboe, and the clarinet; and the brass, for example, the trumpet, the horn and the trombone.

397 The percussion instruments include the drum, the bass drum, the cymbals, the triangle, the tambourine, and sometimes the xylophone.

398 The harp, the lute, the clavichord, and even the organ are added to the orchestra for certain concerts.

399 Some concerts include human voices.

400 If there is only one singer, the piece is called a solo; if there are two or three, it is called a duet or a trio.

401 A choir is made of a large number of singers.

402 Female singers are classified according to the pitch of their voices: the highest are the sopranos, the contraltos are the lowest, and the mezzo-sopranos are in between.

403 It is the register of a soprano's voice which distinguishes her from a mezzo-soprano or a contralto.

404 Most male singers are classified as tenors, baritones and basses according to their register.

405   The highest voices are not necessarily the most beautiful.

406   The principal quality of a voice is its timbre, which reveals the sensitivity of the singer.

407   A good ear is indispensable for a professional singer.

408   In order to be an opera singer one must learn how to breathe in a special way to be able to hold a note for a long time without wavering.

409   To become a good singer it is not enough just to have a good voice; one must work hard and for a long time.

410   Musicians make their instruments vibrate.

411   Each instrument has its own timbre.

412   Several instruments can produce the same note at the same time, but our ear can distinguish them by their timbre.

413   When certain notes are played together and produce a pleasant effect, we say that they harmonize.

414   On the other hand, if they make an unpleasant sound we say they are dissonant or discordant.

415   Some popular songs are sung in a round.

416 A round is a melody, the phrases of which can be superimposed harmoniously. The various voices in the choir take up the same phrases successively; the song can be continued indefinitely.

417 A choir can sing in unison or separate into different voices or parts.

418 American folk music is made up of old songs from the days of exploration and the settling of the various regions of the United States.

419 Popular music has produced thousands of singers and groups of musicians who record their songs to be played on the radio. These musicians appear on television and give live performances as well.

420 America has also produced jazz, which is popular with all age groups in the United States and abroad.

Writing and Painting

421 Although originally American painting drew its inspiration from European painting, in the twentieth century its independence has grown and there are now original modern schools of painting in the United States.

422 One of the best known of these is abstract expressionism.

423   American literature is also prolific and is recognized all over the world.

424   The American language has been greatly enriched by its writers.

425   The American way of life has touched all corners of the world and has been adapted and adopted by many people.

426   The works of many American authors have been translated into scores of languages.

427   In the old days people wrote with a feather, one end of which was sharpened and dipped in ink.

428   The word quill is used for these pens; a quill is the barrel of a feather, the part which is attached to the body of the bird.

429   We can also write or draw with a pencil. The ordinary black pencil is made of graphite, which is surrounded by a strip of wood, often lacquered, and fitted with an eraser at one end.

430   Drawing pencils are made of graphite or charcoal in different grades of thickness and hardness.

431   One can buy lead pencils and colored pencils, or crayons.

432   An eraser is used to rub out mistakes.

433   One uses chalk to write on a chalkboard.

434   A certain type of colored chalk is called pastel.

435   Some painters use pastels in their pictures.

436   Other painters use colored clay.

437   Most painters use oil paints or water colors.

438   For painting in oils a painter uses specially treated canvases. When they are finished the pictures are sometimes varnished.

439   Water colors are done on paper.

440   Pastels and charcoal drawings have to be set with a fixative containing varnish dissolved in acetone.

441   Not all painters are artists.

442   House painters are workers or artisans.

443   They use a big brush or a spray gun to paint the walls.

444   To repaint a wall is to freshen it up.

445   To repaint a picture is to restore it.

446   To restore something is to put it back into its original state. One can restore a picture, a room, an historical building or a political regime.

Toiletry and Beauty Care

447   The verb to refresh oneself has several uses: one refreshes oneself by drinking cold water when one is thirsty; one is refreshed by washing in cold water when one is hot; one can also be refreshed mentally and spiritually by a meeting with congenial people.

448   One also speaks of freshening up, meaning washing, changing clothes, and, for men, shaving.

449   To shave comfortably the blade must be sharp.

450   Most men shave themselves, but some have their barber shave them.

451   Barbers also cut hair; they use scissors and clippers; the clippers may be electric.

452   In some groups, beards, mustaches and longer hair are popular for men.

453 Women's hairdressers use scissors and clippers too and several other implements as well.

454 If one wishes, one can have one's hair shampooed and curled at the hairdresser's.

455 The hairdressers have electric dryers to dry their customers' hair.

456 Clips and rollers are used to curl the hair and keep it in place while it is drying.

457 When it is dry the hairdresser sometimes uses special products, such as hairspray, to help the hairstyle keep its shape.

458 A whole assortment of creams, color rinses, lotions, and perfumes make up the equipment of a ladies' hairdresser.

459 Most hairdressing salons also employ a manicurist, who gives beauty treatments to clients' hands and fingernails and perhaps a pedicurist who cares for the feet and toenails.

460 Most women trim their fingernails, and many put polish on them. Most polishes are red or pink, but they also come in other colors.

461 These days modern homes have one or more bathrooms.

462   One uses soap to wash oneself.

463   The soap is usually perfumed.

464   Depending on family custom one uses a sponge or a face cloth to soap oneself.

465   There are vegetable sponges and artificial ones made of plastic or rubber.

466   To keep one's hair dry under the shower one uses a shower cap, usually made of plastic with elastic edges to keep it tight.

467   In the bathtub one can take a bath and lie and dream.

468   A shower is not so relaxing.

469   One uses a towel to dry oneself.

470   Towels are made of thick absorbent cotton, called terry cloth.

471   Some people have bathrobes made of terry cloth which are used instead of dressing gowns.

472   On the floor beside the bathtub or shower there is a bath mat on which one stands while drying oneself.

473   Some bathrooms have radiators on the wall so that one does not catch a cold.

Clothing

474   The underwear worn by the two sexes is different and varies according to the season.

475   Men wear an undershirt and shorts next to their skin.

476   A woman wears a bra, a slip and panties under her dress.

477   A dress is a one-piece garment.

478   A skirt and slacks are worn with a blouse or sweater.

479   A suit is a two-piece outfit: a skirt and a jacket.

480   Men also wear suits made up of a jacket and a pair of pants.

481   Under the jacket a man may wear a vest.

482   When one goes out in winter, one wears an overcoat as well in order to keep warm.

483   Some overcoats are lined with wool or fur.

484   Some prefer to wear fur on the outside.

485   When it rains, a raincoat is more useful than an overcoat.

486   Winter suits and overcoats are usually made of wool.

487   In summer they may be of cotton or linen or some other light-weight material.

488   Cotton is also used for underwear, handkerchiefs, and shirts.

489   These days nylon, rayon, and other artificial fabrics often replace cotton and silk.

490   Natural silk is still used for materials, but it is not so common now.

491   Because of the growth of the population, artificial fabrics are better, as they can be produced in sufficient quantities at reasonable prices.

492   Fabrics may be multicolored or of one color.

493   They are dyed in all colors, and one can buy printed materials in an enormous variety of shades and designs.

494   Black, gray and navy blue are so-called neutral colors and are worn particularly by people who are no longer very young.

495   Young people prefer bright colors.

496   The length of dresses depends on fashion.

497   So does the position of the waist.

498   Feminine fashions change every year.

499   Men's fashions change too, but not so often.

500   Fashion magazines display the latest styles.

501   High fashion dressmakers are usually called by their French name: couturier.

502   Couturiers employ live models to display their creations.

503   In the windows of shops and stores one sees mannequins made of wax, wood or plastic displaying clothing for women, girls, men and boys.

504   When clothes worn by all people in a group are exactly the same, they are called a uniform.

The Armed Forces

505   Military men normally wear a uniform called fatigues, but they also have a more decorative one for parades.

506   Officers have more elegant uniforms than first class soldiers.

507   They also wear badges and stripes to show their rank.

508   In the army the highest rank is that of General.

509   There are five grades of generals. The highest is a five-star General or General of the Army; he is followed by a four-star General; then a Lieutenant General, who is followed by a Major General and lastly there is the Brigadier General.

510   After the generals come the colonels: a colonel, then a lieutenant-colonel.

511   There are four more officer ranks after a lieutenant-colonel: major, captain, first lieutenant and second lieutenant.

512   In addition to officers and non-commissioned officers (sergeants and corporals), there are also enlisted men and women. They may be specialists or privates.

513   Doctors in the army start with the rank of captain. They may be promoted as high as colonel or even general.

514   The army also has its clergymen. They are called chaplains and are also given the rank of captain.

515   In the Navy the highest rank is that of Admiral.

516   Below the Admiral are the Vice-Admiral and the Rear-Admiral.

517   The person in command of a vessel is called the "Captain," whatever their rank.

518   The Captain, the First Mate, the First Lieutenant and the Quarter-master are all officers concerned with the steering of the ship, the signals, the compass, etc.

519   There are several types of warships: aircraft carriers, cruisers, destroyers, mine sweepers, and submarines.

Navigation

520   There are special names for ships used in the merchant marine.

521   Ships for passengers are called steamships.

522 Ships used for transporting fluids, especially fuel oil, are called tankers.

523 Cargo ships transport other merchandise.

524 Cargo ships load and unload at ports.

525 Cranes are used to lift the cargo from the deck to the ship's hold.

526 In port, cargo ships anchor near the docks.

527 They are moored to the docks by cables, or hawsers, which are looped around and tied to capstans, or rings, which are fixed to the dock.

528 A gangplank connects the ship's deck with the dock for passage from one to the other.

529 Steamships also have engine rooms.

530 These engines usually use heavy-oil fuel.

531 The energy from the combustion of the fuel is used by the turbines to propel the ship.

532 The helm serves to steer the ship.

533 The captain and the first mate steer the ship from the bridge.

534 On all these vessels there is a radio officer who receives and sends messages sometimes in Morse code.

535 Thanks to modern inventions, such as radar and automatic pilot, maritime navigation is less hazardous these days than before.

536 The stability of steamships has also been increased. This has made seasickness, from which many people suffer, less frequent.

Traveling

537 To travel to another country one needs a passport, a visa, and perhaps vaccinations.

538 Visas, entry and exit permits, which are needed for certain countries, are usually stamped in the passport.

539 The dates of the vaccinations required by the international health laws are written on a vaccination certificate.

540   Travelers to some parts of the world must be vaccinated against smallpox.

541   To be admitted to certain countries one must also be vaccinated against yellow fever.

542   For other places vaccination against cholera, typhus, and typhoid are necessary.

543   Illnesses like the plague, diphtheria and malaria are no longer considered a threat to humanity, except when there is an epidemic.

544   The World Health Organization fights against infectious diseases all over the world.

545   The reduction of the mortality rate due to epidemics is one of the big factors in the world population growth during the last decades.

Standard of Living

546   A country's standard of living depends on its wealth and also on its annual rate of population growth.

547   There are many countries in the world where the standard of living is still very low, barely sufficient for mere survival.

548   These are regions where it is difficult to maintain a sufficient level of subsistence.

549   In poor countries the lack of certain foods causes many illnesses.

550   Synthetic vitamins are used to eliminate the symptoms of some of these illnesses.

551   The pharmaceutical industry has made immense progress during this century.

552   This progress is due to scientific discoveries.

553   Everyday scientists are contributing to the advancement of the well being of humanity.

554   New synthetic materials are produced in research laboratories.

555   Because they are synthetic, these materials possess physical properties which are known in advance.

556   Every year new metal alloys appear.

557   New natural phenomena are still being discovered and immediately put to use by man.

558   The universe poses plenty of questions which stimulate man's natural spirit of adventure.

559   It is this ever-curious mind which distinguishes humans from other creatures.

560   The Earth, habitat of human beings, is a planet.

561   The other planets, especially Venus and Mars, attract us, and we wonder if they are also inhabited.

562   Beyond the solar system there are doubtless other similar systems.

563   Beyond our galaxy, which is formed by the Milky Way, there are other galaxies which may have conditions similar to ours.

564   By being able to leave their planet, human beings have enlarged their habitat in an effort to become cosmic.

565   But there are still a great number of problems to be solved on Earth.

The State

566 Politicians belong to political parties.

567 These parties represent the interests of certain groups of citizens.

568 American citizens elect their representatives at local, state and federal levels of government.

569 At the federal level there are senators, who represent whole states, and congressmen who represent districts within a state.

570 There are two houses of Congress, the Senate and the House of Representatives.

571 The name given to state representatives varies across America.

572 At both state and federal levels the elected representatives become members of the Legislature.

573 Members of the Legislature discuss proposed laws which have been submitted by the government or individual members, and vote on them.

574 The Administration accepts or rejects laws passed by the Legislature, and implements those passed. Because of this it is called the Executive Branch of the government.

575 A third branch, the Judiciary, insures that the country is run according to the laws passed by the Congress and accepted by the Executive Branch.

576 Almost all the proceedings in the Legislature are published in an official journal. The record of federal government proceedings is called the "Congressional Record."

577 Each year the state governments and the federal government try to balance their expenses and their revenues.

578 Revenue is derived from direct and indirect taxation.

579 Direct taxation is that levied on personal incomes or on the profits made by commercial corporations.

580 There is an indirect taxation on a number of things.

581 Customs duties, taxes on tobacco and alcohol, sales tax and tax on gasoline are among the principal ones.

582 State and federal governments pay the salaries of their employees and of the people in the Armed Forces. They

also pay for social security, welfare and special projects such as highway construction, dams, etc.

583 The federal government is responsible for the country's defense.

584 State governments pay for education from elementary school to high school and maintain universities; they also contribute to research in specialized fields.

585 Education is actually paid for through local property taxes, and when this is insufficient, the school boards ask for more money by issuing bonds. These are voted on at local election time.

586 Unlike the government of many other countries, the United States Government does not own the railroads, the power supply, or the telecommunications industry.

Agriculture

587 Agriculture is the cultivation of the earth in order to produce food.

588 Farmers and laborers cultivate the earth.

589   They grow grains such as: wheat, corn, barley, oats, and rye.

590   They also grow potatoes, fruits, and vegetables.

591   They raise cattle which graze during the warm months and are kept in barns and stables during the cold months.

592   Cattle give milk and meat.

593   Work in the fields and on farms is becoming more and more mechanized.

594   For a long time horses and mules shared the work of farmers, but they are now rarely used in most parts of the country.

595   Horses are mostly used for riding for pleasure.

596   Other horses are specially bred and trained, and are raced against each other at racetracks.

597   In certain parts of the United States there are very large properties called ranches, where cows and sheep are raised.

598   The migration of people from rural to urban areas has become a big economic problem in the United States and elsewhere.

599   People who work in the country are often attracted by what seem to them to be the advantages of living in a city.

600   On the other hand, urban living is becoming less and less pleasant.

601   Were it not for the scarcity of jobs in the country, modern city life would be enough to discourage many people from moving into the cities.

602   It is difficult to see what will stop this movement of rural people to the cities.

603   American agriculture used to be based on the economy of the small farm.

604   However, increased costs of mechanization have forced many small farmers out of business. Nowadays most farming is done on farms often as large as 5,000 acres.

605   Much of the labor on these huge farms is done by migrant workers, who are paid a small hourly wage.

606   Because these workers are constantly moving from region to region, they are not considered residents of any state. This excludes them from many of the rights of permanent residents.

607 However, the difficulties of living in the country are diminishing each year.

608 Powerful new methods, the results of scientific research, have greatly diminished the risks in agriculture.

609 Artificial fertilizers have raised the yield from the soil and have allowed intensive cultivation.

610 The control of harmful insects and other pests has reduced the damage done to crops, but not to wild life.

611 The selection of grains has improved the varieties available.

612 Refrigeration has reduced spoilage of agricultural products during transportation.

613 Electricity, now accessible almost everywhere in the country, has also reduced the need for manual labor.

614 Means of rapid transportation have brought markets nearer and increased them.

615 The agricultural economy is having a complete revolution.

616 In the cities, automation has reduced the need for unskilled labor.

617   The great buying power of more and more people has raised the number of consumers of industrial products and has made industrialization irreversible.

Sports

618   American society, like that of other developed countries, changes constantly.

619   The time left after working is called leisure time.

620   With economic and technological progress, leisure time is increasing.

621   Sports take up the major part of Americans' leisure time.

622   Those sports where one group or team plays another while other people watch are called spectator sports.

623   The principal spectator sports are football, baseball, basketball, and ice hockey.

624   Many of the larger cities have their own professional teams for these sports.

625   The spectators may pay admission to a stadium to watch a game, or they may watch it on television.

626 Sports vary according to season and climate.

627 Baseball is played in summer, football in fall, ice hockey in winter and basketball in spring.

628 All forms of water sports are extremely popular in the United States.

629 Children usually learn to swim at a very young age.

630 Competitive water sports include swimming, boating and sailing races, water skiing and diving competitions, and water polo matches.

631 Boating and sailing are done at the beach and on the many natural and artificial waterways.

632 One can learn to swim at a public swimming pool.

633 One can also go there on a hot day and swim and dive for fun and to cool off.

634 There are a growing number of private swimming pools.

635 Tennis, bowling, and golf are also very popular forms of exercise; they may be hobbies or competitive sports.

636 Competitions range from small local contests to nationwide tournaments for amateurs or professionals.

637   In most cities the YMCA and YWCA, the young men's and women's Christian associations, have facilities for sports and hobbies at a low cost.

638   There are also thousands of country clubs situated in and around towns, where facilities exist for many sports, including swimming, tennis and golf.

639   Members of these clubs pay a subscription to belong and have the right to the facilities. Clubs also provide bars and dining rooms.

640   Skating and skiing are the most popular winter sports.

641   Skiing facilities in the United States are excellent with many choices of trails at different levels of difficulty.

642   Many resorts have equipment for making artificial snow, in case it does not fall naturally, and floodlights to make night skiing possible.

643   There are skiing competitions, testing speed and skill, and also jumping contests.

644   Athletics and track events are usually competitive, the top people being chosen for places in teams which compete in the Olympic Games.

645   Fishing is one of the most popular forms of relaxation for Americans.

646   Fishing in the oceans for salmon, tuna, marlin, and other deep-sea fishing is a very exciting sport.

647   Inland fishing from boats or the water's edge is more available to everyone.

648   Skin-diving and underwater fishing are also growing in popularity.

649   From a very early age Americans are encouraged to play some sort of sport, and the climate and facilities allow most people to continue their sporting interests later as adults.

Immigration

650   Most of the original settlers of the United States came from Great Britain and Western European countries.

651   Those who ran plantations in the southern states imported African slaves to work for them.

652   After emancipation from slavery these black people began to leave their rural homes.

653   Some moved to the urban centers of the south; others went to cities in other parts of the country.

654   In more recent years, there has been a great immigration of peoples from the countries of Eastern Europe, Italy, Greece, Japan, China, and South and Central America.

655   In the early years of these large immigrations most of the people settled in the urban centers near their port of entry.

656   They lived with other people from their native countries in neighborhoods where they could preserve their languages and cultural styles.

657   Some of the children of these immigrants moved away from their old neighborhoods to settle in various parts of the United States.

658   Often they preserved fewer of the old traditions.

659   Now it is possible to find people of all national backgrounds everywhere in the United States.

660   Their various life-styles have influenced the culture of other Americans, particularly their food and music.

661   Gradually, American society is expanding to include these people in its social and political life.

Working at Night

662   While most people work in offices during the daytime, there are many people who work at night or work on rotating work schedules, called shifts.

663   If the job has to be manned twenty-four hours a day, there are usually three shifts of eight hours in a day.

664   Many positions connected with public services have shift schedules.

665   Hospitals have shifts for their doctors, nurses, and other personnel.

666   The police, the fire department, ambulance services, and other public aid groups work around-the-clock, seven days a week.

667   Power plants, telephone companies, and some construction and repair jobs also operate day and night.

668   Doormen and security guards work at night.

669   Smaller food stores are often open twenty hours a day.

670   Hotels, restaurants, cafes, and bars all need to employ people to work at night.

671   Radio stations often broadcast twenty-four hours a day, and some television channels only close down for four or five hours a day.

672   Taxis and other public transportation are available during the night in big cities and until quite late in smaller towns.

673   Gas stations usually have an all-night attendant.

674   Airports stay open all night, though there is usually not much traffic between three and six in the morning.

675   Bakers have to be up early to prepare their goods, and grocers and butchers usually go to early morning markets to buy their produce.

Seas and Rivers

676   A beach is a region beside the sea.

677   In summer if it is nice, the beaches are full of bathers.

678   The sand at the beach varies from very fine to quite coarse.

679   The water on the shore comes in at high tide and goes out at low tide.

680   The cycle of the tide occurs twice every 24 hours and is dependent on the moon.

681   The extent of the water's recession and influx varies with the topography of the coast and with the seasons.

682   Rivers flow into the sea or the ocean.

683   Often smaller rivers flow into other rivers.

684   The water in rivers is called fresh water.

685   Sea water is called salt water.

686   Rivers form a delta when they divide into several branches to flow into the sea.

687   The mouth of a waterway is the place where it flows into the sea or into another waterway.

688   The water close to the mouth of a river which flows into the sea is called brackish, partly salt and partly fresh.

689   When the mouth of a river forms a deep gulf it is called an estuary.

690   The bottom of a river is called its bed.

691   When the water of a river is polluted, one must not drink
       it.

692   In regions where there is insufficient rainwater for
       agriculture, the fields are irrigated by water from the
       rivers.

693   If a boat can sail up a river, the river is said to be
       navigable.

Cleaning and Laundry

694   Modern chemical industry has produced detergents.

695   Detergents are preferred to soap for washing large
       amounts of things. They lather easily and take out the
       dirt.

696   But they produce pollution of rivers and are less popular
       nowadays.

697   Washing walls, floors, dishes, and sometimes curtains,
       rugs, etc. are big jobs for which strong cleaning materials
       are used.

698   But to wash delicate materials, most people prefer soap.

699   After being washed, the articles must be dried.

700   After drying they usually need to be ironed.

701   Nowadays there are materials which do not need to be ironed to look neat.

702   Certain materials and clothes should not be washed; they must be dry-cleaned.

703   Some fabrics, like fur and leather, must be treated specially.

704   Most dry-cleaners also dye fabrics.

705   Materials sold in stores have already been dyed in the factory where they were produced.

706   Most modern fabrics are colorfast, which means the color will not run when the article is washed.

707   Sometimes fabrics do lose their color, especially those from countries which are less advanced industrially.

708   Colors fade if they are exposed for a long time to the sun's rays.

709   They discolor under the effects of chemical reactions, as is the case when they have contact with perspiration.

Relaxation

710   Some colors absorb more of the sun's rays than others.

711   In hot countries and during the hot season elsewhere, people prefer to wear white.

712   White clothing reflects most of the sun's rays.

713   Cotton is well suited to the same conditions.

714   Silk and artificial fabrics are better suited to cold climates or to being worn during the cold season.

715   A white cotton dress in winter would be as uncomfortable as a dress of black wool in the middle of summer.

716   Each season requires certain clothes, underwear, and a way of wearing them.

717   In the southern parts of the United States even winter is not very cold, but in the north the winter can be very severe.

718   Fashion introduced the two-piece bathing suit for women.

719   Tiny two-piece suits are called bikinis.

720   Men wear shorts as a bathing suit and have their torsos bare.

721   Often on the beach one takes shelter from the sun under an umbrella.

722   The eyes are protected by sunglasses.

723   Sun-bathing, lying in the sun in order to have one's skin tanned, is very popular in the United States but is not without dangerous consequences.

724   One can also get a tan artificially by using a special oil on the skin before going into the sun.

725   The best physical refreshment comes from the complete relaxation of one's body during a nap.

726   It is more relaxing to take a nap on a lounge than in an armchair. People put lounges outside in their gardens as well as in houses.

727   Sleeping takes up a good third of most people's life.

728   Napping is not sleeping soundly.

729   It is rather the lack of consciousness for a short period.

730   The opposite of being asleep is being awake.

731   To wake up is to leave sleep.

732   Some people wake up very early and others very late in the day.

733   One also says of a bright, intelligent child that he is awake; it is another use of the word, a figurative one.

734   When someone is slow in understanding a joke or the point of a remark, we say to him: "Wake up!"

Feelings

735   When everything is going well we say that we are happy.

736   Unhappiness is the opposite of happiness.

737   When one is unhappy, one sighs and laments or even cries.

738   When one is happy one is calm or one smiles and sings.

739   One may be unhappy for all sorts of reasons:

740   Because one has had an argument with a friend.

741   Or because one has quarreled with a neighbor or with a relative.

742   Because one has lost all one's money or simply because one has lost something one had and valued.

743   Or because one is suffering physically;

744   Or because one has been deceived or disappointed.

745   Everyone suffers when wronged.

746   Death always takes us by surprise, even though we know it is inevitable.

747   To express sympathy to someone who is suffering is to share his sorrow.

748   We send condolences to those whose friend or close relative has died.

Accidents and Wounds

749   Certain collective disasters cause more than personal suffering.

750   An earthquake is a disaster, a natural catastrophe.

751   Tidal waves are often a consequence of earthquakes.

752   Floods come after torrential rains.

753   Tornados, cyclones, and hurricanes, which occur regularly in some areas, are also natural calamities.

754   Hail can ruin harvests.

755   Drought often brings famine.

756   Grasshoppers and locusts are permanent plagues in some areas of the world.

757   Swarms of locusts, like great clouds, move over long distances and devastate immense areas of crops.

758   Mosquitoes are another plague.

759   A mosquito bite irritates the skin, and certain species of mosquito leave the body infected with a malarial microbe. These mosquitoes only inhabit certain parts of the world.

760   Fleas live on the blood supply of animals and humans.

761   Lice, which do not jump like fleas, prefer to live in the hairy parts of the body, especially in the hair on the head.

762   Bedbugs are also parasites; they live in the cracks of beds and feed on the blood of sleeping people.

763   Flies are found in great numbers, especially during the warm season in most parts of the world.

764   They carry illnesses and transport germs from one place to another.

On Bees and Wax

765   Bees, wasps, and gnats carry on the hair of their legs pollen, which they gather from flowers.

766   This pollen is used to fertilize monosexual or bisexual flowers.

767   Bees are attracted by the perfume or nectar of certain flowers.

768   The sting of a bee or a wasp is very painful.

769   These stings can be treated with ammonia.

770   Bees make honey.

771   The honey is stored in wax cells, called hives.

772   Bee-keepers collect the honey and sell it.

773   The wax is used to make shoe polish.

774   Shoeshine stands are becoming less common now.

775   To polish shoes one needs two brushes, one for putting on the polish and the other for rubbing the leather until it shines.

776   A piece of velvet gives a final touch to the shine.

777   Candles are also made of wax.

778   Candles are used in religious ceremonies and for decoration in homes.

779   In religious ceremonies candles are lit at certain times as an offering on the altar or for a vigil in a ceremony for the dead.

780   To put out big candles, one uses a snuffer.

781   To light candles, one uses matches.

782   Safety matches are struck against a strip of rough material made of phosphorus and rubber.

Smoking

783   Some smokers prefer to use a lighter instead of matches.

784   Lighters use gas or fluid.

785   The wick of the lighter is soaked in highly inflammable fluid.

786   A rough wheel rubs against the flint and produces a spark which ignites the fluid.

787   Pipe smokers may use a lighter to relight their pipes, which go out easily.

788   Cigarettes are made of tobacco rolled in paper.

789   Cigars are leaves of tobacco rolled together.

790   The end of a cigarette or a cigar which is not smoked is called the butt.

791   When tobacco is burned, it becomes ash.

792   Ashtrays are used for depositing ashes and butts.

793   Cigarettes are sold in packs; cigars, singly or in a box.

794   Pipe smokers buy their tobacco in a packet or a tin.

795   Some smokers use a cigarette case.

796   Tobacco contains nicotine and other harmful products.

797   In spite of this, many people still smoke.

Drinking

798   The habit of drinking alcohol to excess is considered a vice.

799   It is difficult to give up the habits of drinking and smoking.

800   Those who often drink too much and do not know how to stop themselves are called alcoholics.

801   Someone who gets drunk occasionally cannot be called an alcoholic.

802   One can drink in bars and nightclubs.

803   Many restaurants serve drinks with food.

804   Beer is very popular in the United States, but some people drink wine with their dinner.

805   Many brands of whisky are available; these and other liquors are also drunk before and with meals.

806   A martini is one of many popular American cocktails; it is very strong.

807   Most wine is imported to the United States from Europe, but there is a growing domestic production, particularly in California and New York State.

808   Hard liquor has a higher alcohol content than beer or wine.

809   American whisky and beer are exported all over the world.

810   The time when the vines are harvested to make wine is called vintage time.

811   The juice from the grapes is fermented in vats.

812   The wine is bottled before it is sold.

813   Each bottle has a cork.

814   The brand mark and year of production are printed on the label.

815   As a rule a well-sealed bottle should last indefinitely without the wine turning sour.

Trains and Stations

816   The transportation of liquids is done by train, in tank cars, or by road, in tank trucks.

817   A train used for carrying passengers is made up of a line of cars or coaches.

818   Those used for carrying animals have stock cars, and those used for carrying other produce are made up of freight cars.

819   All trains are pulled by one or more engines.

820   Steam engines were operated by two people: the engineer, who drives the machine and watches the tracks and the signals, and the fireman, who keeps the furnace supplied with coal.

821   Most modern engines do not run on steam. There is no fireman, and the engineer is called a driver.

822   In the cab of the engine there are a number of instruments which the driver manipulates or consults:

823   The brakes, which stop the train or slow it down;

824   The thermometer shows the temperature of the engine, and the speedometer the speed at which the train is going;

825   The knobs for the windshield wipers, ventilation, and the whistle;

826   The odometer which tells how many miles have been covered;

827   A manual accelerator, which is used to vary the speed of the engine.

828   Some of these instruments are also found in cars, in the cockpits of planes, and in the engine room of ships.

829   The rails are part of the tracks.

830   The rails are kept parallel by means of ties.

831 The ties are made of wood, or metal, or reinforced concrete, depending on the use the railroad gets.

832 Between the ties and rails there are small stones packed together.

833 The embankment on which the railroad is put is compressed and reinforced in order to be able to take the weight of trains.

834 An overhead road for cars or railroads is called a viaduct.

835 A track which runs over a river is more usually called a railroad bridge.

836 Semaphore signals are used to tell the driver if the line is clear or not.

837 Express trains are those which only stop at important stations.

838 Freight trains and passenger trains which are slower are sometimes moved onto a siding in order to allow an express train to pass.

839 At the stations, the platform usually faces more than one track.

840 The station master is the highest officer at the station.

841   He may have one or more employees under him, depending on the importance of the station.

842   At the station there is a place where one can leave one's baggage for a few hours or even longer.

843   The clerks at the baggage check put the suitcases on racks, which have numbers corresponding to the numbers on the tickets they give to the owners.

844   Nowadays more and more stations have lockers where one can leave baggage without the help of a clerk.

845   At all important stations there is a restaurant.

846   Some restaurants have only a counter where one stands and eats; some others, a counter where one can sit; and others have tables and chairs.

847   At the restaurant the travelers can buy sandwiches, fruit, and drinks, which can be eaten there or taken out to be eaten later on the train.

848   At most stations one can also buy something to read.

849   Sometimes there is a complete book store, sometimes just a magazine and newspaper stand.

850   If one is traveling with luggage, it is usually placed on a rack above one's seat, though on a few trains there are luggage compartments; the bigger ones are called baggage cars, and are for bags and trunks only.

Shopping

851   Americans like to go shopping by car as this is the most convenient way to take home purchases.

852   Parking space in the crowded downtown streets is scarce, and parking lots where one pays by the hour are often inconveniently located.

853   Shopping centers, groups of stores next to large free parking lots, cater to shoppers who drive.

854   These are usually located on major roads in the suburbs or on highways near country towns.

855   The smallest shopping centers have five or six businesses, located adjacent to each other in a long building.

856   Usually they have a gas station, a supermarket, and a drugstore.

857   There may also be a bank, a dollar store, clothing stores, restaurants and other specialty shops.

858   The largest shopping centers are elaborate malls, housing as many as sixty businesses or more.

859   Sometimes one large discount store will serve as an entire shopping center.

860   These discount stores sell hardware, household appliances, and non-prescription drugs for lower prices than regular retail stores.

861   They also sell inexpensive cosmetics, stationery, clothing, and shoes, but these items are not marked down.

Post Offices and Mail

862   In some railroad stations there are post offices, and in all stations there are telephone booths.

863   At post offices one buys stamps, leaves registered letters, sends parcels or money orders, etc.

864   City post offices have a special window where one can collect mail which has been sent care of that office. This window is marked General Delivery.

865   Some people have their mail sent to a post office.

866   These people rent a box at the post office and have a key for it.

867   Mail carriers distribute letters and parcels to homes.

868   In the streets at regular intervals there are mail boxes where one can put letters to be sent.

869   These mail boxes are emptied at set times during the day and evening.

870   The mail is sorted at the post offices before being distributed.

871   Then it is sent to its destination by different ways provided by the postal administration.

872   Airmail letters have to be taken to airports by train or truck.

873   The cost of postage is fixed by the Postmaster General in accordance with the government.

874   Many commemorative stamps are put into circulation during each year by the postal administration.

875   Stamp collectors are called philatelists.

876   They collect their stamps in albums.

877   Some rare stamps have enormous value for collectors.

878   These days collectors specialize in the stamps of a few countries.

879   Stamps which have been postmarked have greater value than new ones.

880   Usually letters are put in envelopes.

881   Envelopes are sealed by glue; one has to moisten the part which has already had glue put on it for it to stick to the other side when folded.

882   Addresses are written on one side of the envelope.

883   In the United States addresses are written as follows: first the name of the receiver, preceded by Mr., Ms. (Mrs. or Miss), or the title of the person: Doctor, Professor, Senator, etc. Then comes the actual address: the number of the house and the name of the street; below that, the name of the town and the state and finally the zip code.

884   If necessary, "airmail" is added and additional stamps, for which one must pay extra postage.

885   If one wants to register a letter, it has to be taken to a post office, and a slip, called a receipt, has to be filled out.

886   This receipt, which is stamped and dated, is kept by the sender and is only used if the letter is lost or not delivered correctly.

887   "Special delivery" letters are those which are delivered immediately by a messenger when they arrive in the town of their destination.

888   These messengers ride bicycles or motorcycles.

889   In most cities in the United States mail is delivered once a day at more or less the same time each day.

890   The mail carrier carries the mail in a bag from house to house.

891   The mail has already been sorted at the post office according to streets and ordered by street numbers.

892   In the cities where there are huge apartment blocks with hundreds of families in the same building, the mail for each block is delivered by truck.

893   Then the mail carrier goes from building to building, putting the letters into the private mail boxes.

Telephone

894 The telephone system in the United States is run by various private corporations.

895 Cellular phone services are also privately owned and are sometimes separate from the telephone services.

896 To use a public telephone, one needs certain coins depending on whether one is making a local call or a long distance call, and depending also on how long one wishes to speak.

897 Cell phones allow one to communicate through text messaging and email, sometimes for an additional fee.

898 On the phone keypad, there are numbers and letters. To get information or assistance one dials zero for the operator.

899 Many operators have been replaced by machines.

900 To answer a telephone one lifts the receiver and says, "Hello."

901 If it is a business phone, one usually says the name of the business or institution and sometimes "good morning," or "good afternoon" as well.

902   At the end of a conversation one may say "goodbye" before hanging up.

903   Telephone systems form an international network, which reach more and more countries. These days one can call almost anywhere in the world from one's own home.

904   Long distance phone calls require you to dial a country code.

905   Thanks to artificial satellites, the natural obstacles to the reception of radio-diffused signals have been overcome.

906   Electronic progress is enabling an ever-increasing number of forms for communication.

907   A trans-Pacific or a trans-Atlantic phone call can be as clear as a local call.

908   It is also possible to make a phone call through the computer,

909   Or one can receive an email through one's cell phone.

910   People still enjoy receiving letters in the mail.

Correspondence

911   American letters begin and end in certain ways.

912   Business correspondence and other formal letters follow a particular format. The address of the writer and date go in the top right-hand corner of the page.

913   Lower down on the left side one puts the name or the title and the address of the person to whom the letter is being written.

914   If the name of the person being addressed is not known, one writes To Whom it May Concern after the heading.

915   One ends this type of letter by writing Sincerely.

916   When one writes to someone whose name is known, one begins by writing, Dear Mr. ... or Dear Ms. ..., and ends by writing Sincerely yours, Yours truly, or, less formally, Regards.

917   Letters written to friends do not have such a formal heading. One simply writes the date in the upper right-hand corner and starts the letter with Dear...

918   One can end this type of letter in many ways. Two of the more common ways are simply to sign one's name, or to write Love and then sign one's name.

919 Many different openings and closings are used in more intimate letters, according to the relationship between the people involved. Here there are no rules to follow.

News and the Press

920 In America freedom of the press is guaranteed by the First Amendment to the U.S. Constitution.

921 All cities have at least one daily newspaper, often more.

922 Newspapers not only inform the public but comment on the happenings in the country and abroad.

923 In the daily papers there are articles in depth as well as advertisements and the news of the day.

924 Most daily newspapers and weekly, monthly, bimonthly, and quarterly journals and magazines have a particular point of view, which is linked to the views of their editors or their publishers.

925 These views are expressed in special articles called editorials.

926 In matters of politics, art, and religion, opinions are sharply divided.

927   Online news has become a very popular source of information in North America.

928   In most countries there is a censor or board of censors, which can prevent something from being published or a film from being shown to the public at large.

929   During times of crisis there may also be censorship.

930   Radio and television programs are carefully prepared in advance.

931   The programs are announced in newspapers and in special program guides.

932   Stations broadcast popular and classical music; occasionally, entire concerts are broadcast as well as opera, plays and ballets; usually certain radio stations or television channels specialize in these programs.

933   They also put on lectures or talks, conversations, interviews, and discussions which are centered around some topics of timely interest.

On Laughter

934   There are many ways of laughing.

935 We burst out laughing when we are very amused, as when we watch a comedy act or when we hear a joke.

936 We smile when we are pleasantly surprised.

937 We smile when we are pleased, and we laugh when we are amused.

938 Laughter can be cruel.

939 Sometimes people laugh from shock instead of crying.

940 One can laugh until one cries if one laughs too much.

941 Funny stories make us laugh or giggle.

942 Puns, plays on words, also make us laugh.

943 Magazines and newspapers publish drawings, called cartoons, whose appearance or content make us laugh.

944 On radio and television there are programs in which comedians tell anecdotes or make jokes to amuse the audience.

945 Some comedians are very popular with the public, and their appearance on a program is a great attraction.

946   Famous actors and show business people are paid very highly for an appearance.

Money

947   Money is used as a medium of exchange.

948   With money one can buy products or go to a theater or contribute to a good cause.

949   To be rich is to have enough money to buy almost anything one wants.

950   Most people are not rich.

951   Not to have even enough money to buy the things one needs is to be poor.

952   To be poor also means to be unable to have the things one wants.

953   Although there are not many rich people, in technologically advanced countries, there are more and more people who are comfortably well off.

954 The middle class in society is made up of people who have enough money for their needs and some other things which are useful, but not needed.

955 These days people are classed mostly according to their income. The lowest class is made up of those who are destitute or on welfare.

956 Formerly they were classed according to their birth, which sometimes was synonymous with wealth.

957 Nobility and aristocracy are references to birth, not to wealth.

958 Someone who has recently become rich is said to be "nouveau riche." The phrase is pejorative.

959 One may become rich suddenly through speculating and playing the stock market, or by winning a lottery, or by gambling.

960 At the stock exchanges, shares and stock in public corporations are sold, as well as government bonds.

961 The value of stocks fluctuates constantly and depends on the state of the national economy and on the success of the particular concern.

962   Stockbrokers direct the stock exchange and buy and sell for their clients.

963   They charge a commission on each transaction.

964   Their clients are the owners, or holders, of the stocks.

965   There are thousands of corporations whose shares are quoted on the stock exchange.

966   In New York alone, millions of stocks are traded everyday.

967   Special newspapers inform speculators and stock brokers of trading and trends in the economy.

968   Apart from commercial stocks, the government also issues stocks and bonds in its enterprises.

969   If a corporation is making money, it issues a dividend. This is interest on the money invested in the corporation by the stockholder.

970   In complex economies there are thousands of ways of accumulating wealth.

971   Wealth in a country is produced by industry which relies on the exploitation of the products deep in the earth: the metals, the minerals, oil, coal, etc., by controlling natural sources of energy; by making roads for commercial

transportation, and by opening airports and attracting visitors.

972   The present world can steadily increase its wealth and seriously contemplate a time when poverty will have been overcome.

Animals and Pets

973   Americans keep many different animals as pets.

974   Goldfish and guppies are the hardiest and most common of the many varieties of fish which people keep in small indoor aquariums or fishbowls.

975   Birds, too, are popular as domestic pets.

976   Some birds are pretty to look at, and some are kept because they sing sweetly.

977   Parrots and parakeets can be let out of their cages and may be tamed, handled, and trained to talk.

978   Canaries can be very good songsters.

979   There is a huge variety of dogs and cats which people keep as pets.

980   Until dogs are six months old they are called puppies; young cats are called kittens.

981   Dogs and cats may have pedigrees, which means they are pure-bred, with registered lineage.

982   The owner of a well-trained dog may enter him in a dog show.

983   A dog that is a mixture of several breeds is called a mutt.

984   Even in small apartments, people keep large dogs which have to be walked daily.

985   Cats are usually more suited to apartment dwelling because they do not need to be exercised.

986   In most cities there are laws requiring people to keep their dogs confined by fences or chains and to walk them on a leash.

987   A dog-catcher is employed by the city to pick up stray animals.

988   They are taken to the pound, where they are kept a certain number of days, then given away or "put to sleep."

989   In the country, there is more room for larger animals.

990   People may own a horse or even have a farm animal as a pet.

991   Some varieties of rodents are considered good pets for children, namely, white mice, hamsters, guinea pigs, and gerbils.

The Future

992   Although not without difficult problems, the future is very promising.

993   The conquest of deserts, the de-pollution of the whole planet, the peaceful exploitation of nuclear energy and of applied sciences are in the process of transforming one's vision of oneself and the world.

994   Thus, today human beings know themselves as being in the process of transformation.

995   We are changing and changing our environment.

996   The decades to come are not simply going to repeat the past.

997   Our libraries will no longer contain only great works of imagination and those that describe the human conquests.

998   Books of inspiration will replace those which amuse us.

999   School will become a window onto the universe.

1,000   All our talents will be developed.

1,001   Instead of speaking only one language, we will be able to know as many as we wish.

www.ingramcontent.com/pod-product-compliance
Lightning Source LLC
LaVergne TN
LVHW061226060426
835509LV00012B/1439